A Sports Illustrated For Kids Book

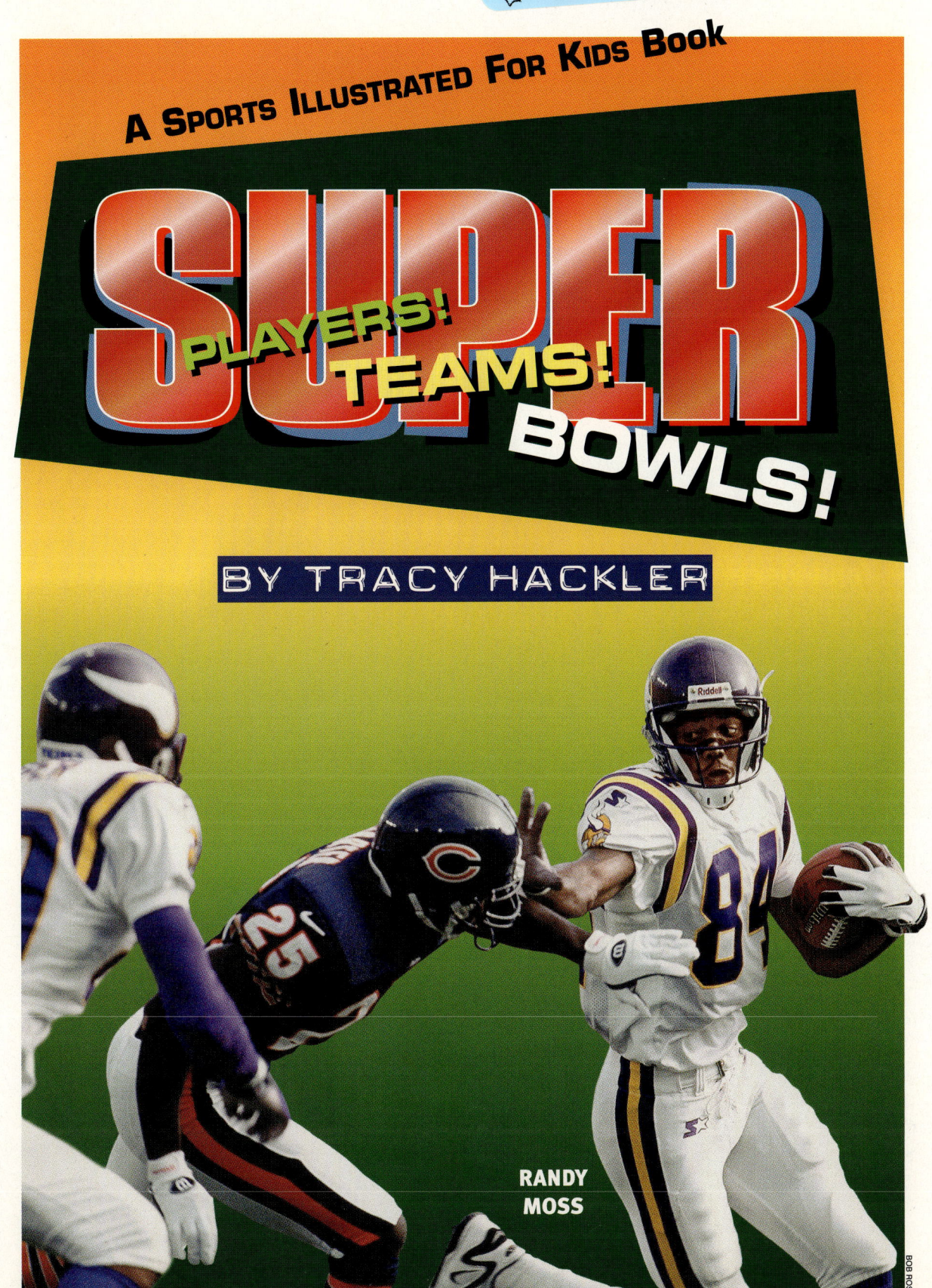

SUPER
Players! Teams! Bowls!

By Tracy Hackler

RANDY MOSS

BOB ROSATO

SUPER PLAYERS!

SUPER

CONTENTS

INTRODUCTION 4
SUPER PLAYERS
  Super Passers 6
  Super Catchers 8
  Super Runners 10
  Super Stoppers 12
SUPER TEAMS
  St. Louis Rams 14
  Tennessee Titans 16
  Indianapolis Colts 18
  Jacksonville Jaguars 19
  Tampa Bay Buccaneers 20
  Washington Redskins 21
SUPER BOWLS
  Super Bowl XXXIV/2000 22
  Super Bowl XXXII/1998 26
  Super Bowl XXX/1996 28
  Super Bowl XXIX/1995 30
FUN FACTS 32

DEHOOG/TDP

KEYSHAWN JOHNSON

The Bucs acquired Keyshawn to help their offense. Their defense was already awesome!

TEAMS! SUPER BOWLS!

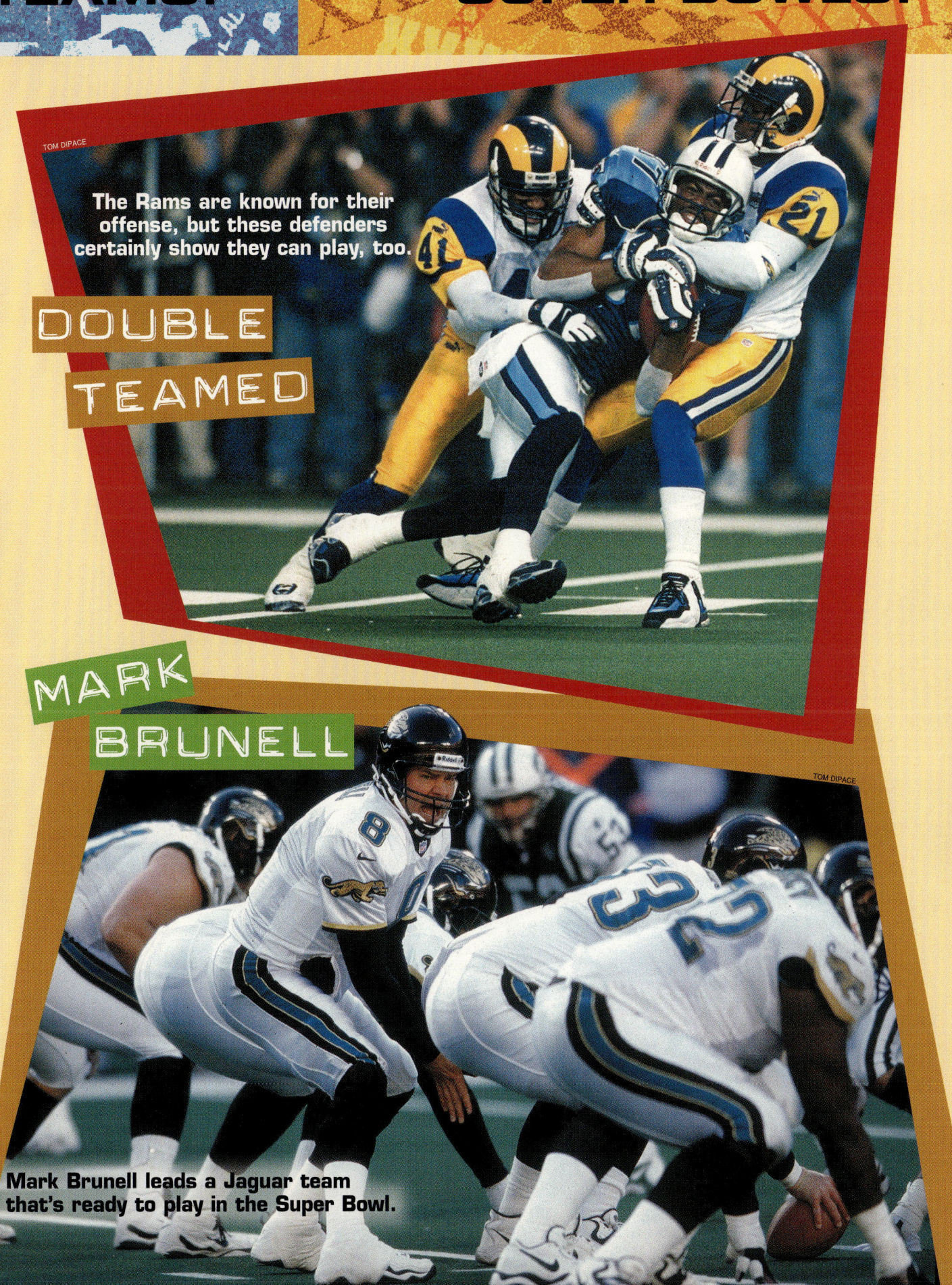

The Rams are known for their offense, but these defenders certainly show they can play, too.

DOUBLE TEAMED

MARK BRUNELL

Mark Brunell leads a Jaguar team that's ready to play in the Super Bowl.

SUPER PLAYERS! SUPER

Great players making great plays — like Ricky Watters catching this pass in Super Bowl XXIX — is only part of what the NFL's championship game is all about.

DAMIAN STROHMEYER/SPORTS ILLUSTRATED

TEAMS!

SUPER BOWLS!

INTRODUCTION

It's Super Bowl time!

Each year, more than 1,600 NFL players strive to reach the biggest event in all of sports. They start preparing for it — sweating, struggling, bleeding, and building — in February, so that they can be ready the next January . . . *if* their team makes it that far.

These players make their living trying to get to the Super Bowl, knowing all the time that most players never do. Through 2000, only 22 of the NFL's 31 teams had even played in the Super Bowl. Just 14 teams had ever won it! Of the 1,600 players who start the season with Super Bowl dreams, only 50 or so will get to walk away with championship rings.

The Super Bowl is the greatest, most anticipated single sporting event in America. More than 132 million Americans watch the game on TV. They all want to see which players will emerge as heroes, what "miracles" may occur, and what dreams will be dashed.

Fans certainly saw heroes emerge and dreams dashed in Super Bowl XXXIV, played between the St. Louis Rams and the Tennessee Titans, in January 2000. Neither team had won a Super Bowl before. Both fought hard, and, in the end, the game was decided on the very last play! Turn to the "Super Bowls" chapter of this book *(page 22)* and you can read about that play, and other great plays from the greatest games in Super Bowl history.

In "Super Players" and "Super Teams," you can check out some of the amazing players who have Super Bowl dreams. When the 2000-01 season kicked off, these guys all had one date marked on their calendar: January 28, 2001 — the date of Super Bowl XXXV.

No matter who makes it to the Super Bowl, two things are certain: First, America will watch with fascination. Second, the NFL superstars on the following pages, and the teams they lead, will have a hand in determining the outcome of the biggest sports event of the year, the Super Bowl.

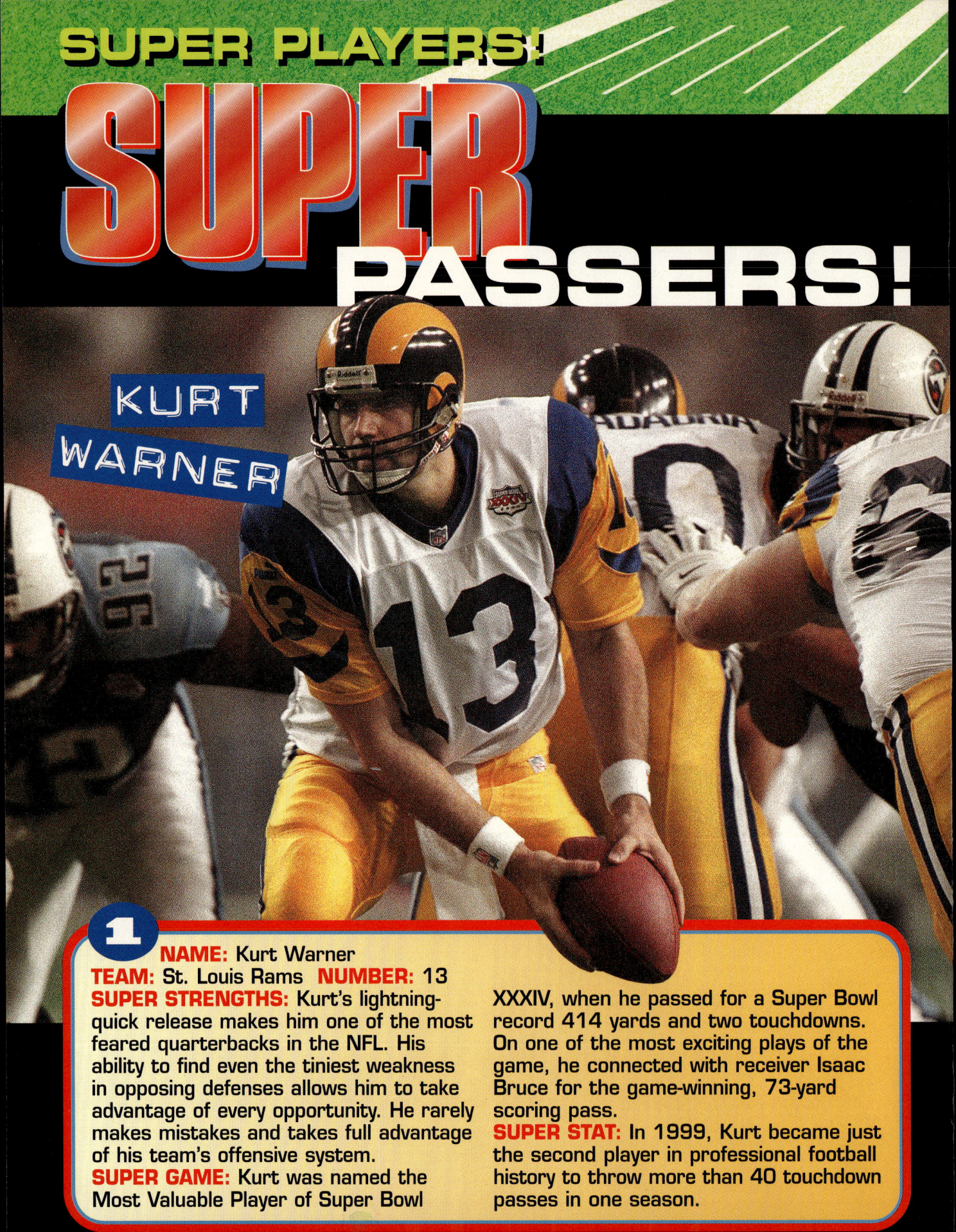

SUPER PLAYERS!
SUPER PASSERS!

KURT WARNER

1

NAME: Kurt Warner
TEAM: St. Louis Rams **NUMBER:** 13
SUPER STRENGTHS: Kurt's lightning-quick release makes him one of the most feared quarterbacks in the NFL. His ability to find even the tiniest weakness in opposing defenses allows him to take advantage of every opportunity. He rarely makes mistakes and takes full advantage of his team's offensive system.
SUPER GAME: Kurt was named the Most Valuable Player of Super Bowl XXXIV, when he passed for a Super Bowl record 414 yards and two touchdowns. On one of the most exciting plays of the game, he connected with receiver Isaac Bruce for the game-winning, 73-yard scoring pass.
SUPER STAT: In 1999, Kurt became just the second player in professional football history to throw more than 40 touchdown passes in one season.

PEYTON MANNING

2

NAME: Peyton Manning
TEAM: Indianapolis Colts   **NUMBER:** 18
SUPER STRENGTHS: Much of Peyton's success begins off the field. He studies lots of game film and gains knowledge from his father, Archie, who was an NFL quarterback for 13 years. Peyton stands a whopping 6-foot 5-inches tall. Being so tall enables him to look over the offensive and defensive linemen in front of him.
SUPER STATS: During his first year as a professional, in 1998, Peyton established NFL rookie records for completions (326), yards (3,739), touchdowns (26), and consecutive games with a TD pass (13).

3

NAME: Brett Favre
TEAM: Green Bay Packers   **NUMBER:** 4
SUPER STRENGTHS: Brett is at his best on the run, making terrific, magical plays when there seems to be no play at all to make. He's one of the toughest quarterbacks in the league and almost never misses games due to injury.
SUPER GAME: Brett thrilled everyone during Super Bowl XXXI. He tossed two long touchdown passes (54 yards to Andre Rison and 81 yards to Antonio Freeman) and ran for a score in Green Bay's 35–21 win over the New England Patriots.

BRETT FAVRE

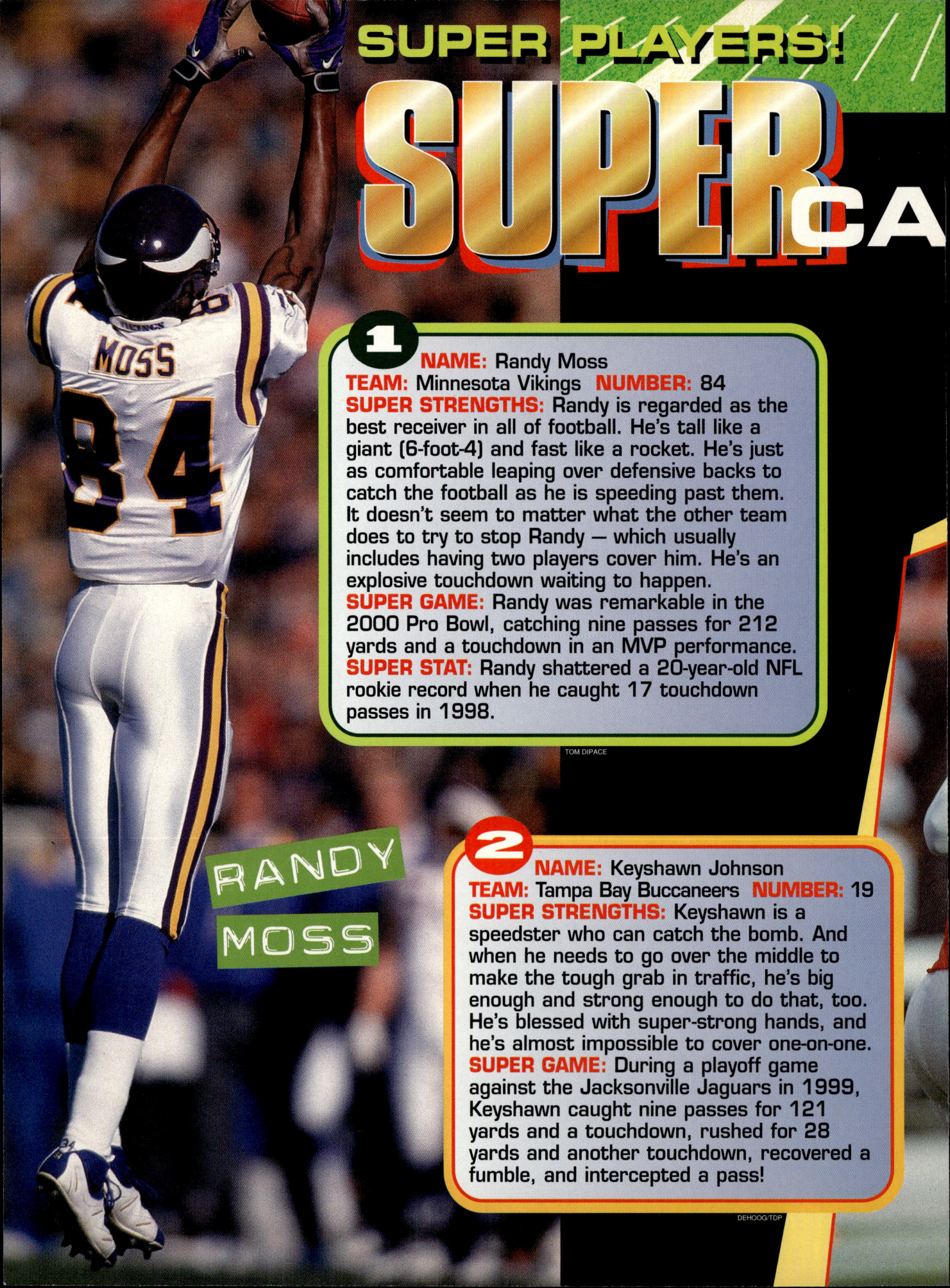

SUPER PLAYERS!
SUPER CA

1
NAME: Randy Moss
TEAM: Minnesota Vikings **NUMBER:** 84
SUPER STRENGTHS: Randy is regarded as the best receiver in all of football. He's tall like a giant (6-foot-4) and fast like a rocket. He's just as comfortable leaping over defensive backs to catch the football as he is speeding past them. It doesn't seem to matter what the other team does to try to stop Randy — which usually includes having two players cover him. He's an explosive touchdown waiting to happen.
SUPER GAME: Randy was remarkable in the 2000 Pro Bowl, catching nine passes for 212 yards and a touchdown in an MVP performance.
SUPER STAT: Randy shattered a 20-year-old NFL rookie record when he caught 17 touchdown passes in 1998.

TOM DIPACE

RANDY MOSS

2
NAME: Keyshawn Johnson
TEAM: Tampa Bay Buccaneers **NUMBER:** 19
SUPER STRENGTHS: Keyshawn is a speedster who can catch the bomb. And when he needs to go over the middle to make the tough grab in traffic, he's big enough and strong enough to do that, too. He's blessed with super-strong hands, and he's almost impossible to cover one-on-one.
SUPER GAME: During a playoff game against the Jacksonville Jaguars in 1999, Keyshawn caught nine passes for 121 yards and a touchdown, rushed for 28 yards and another touchdown, recovered a fumble, and intercepted a pass!

DEHOOG/TDP

TCHERS!

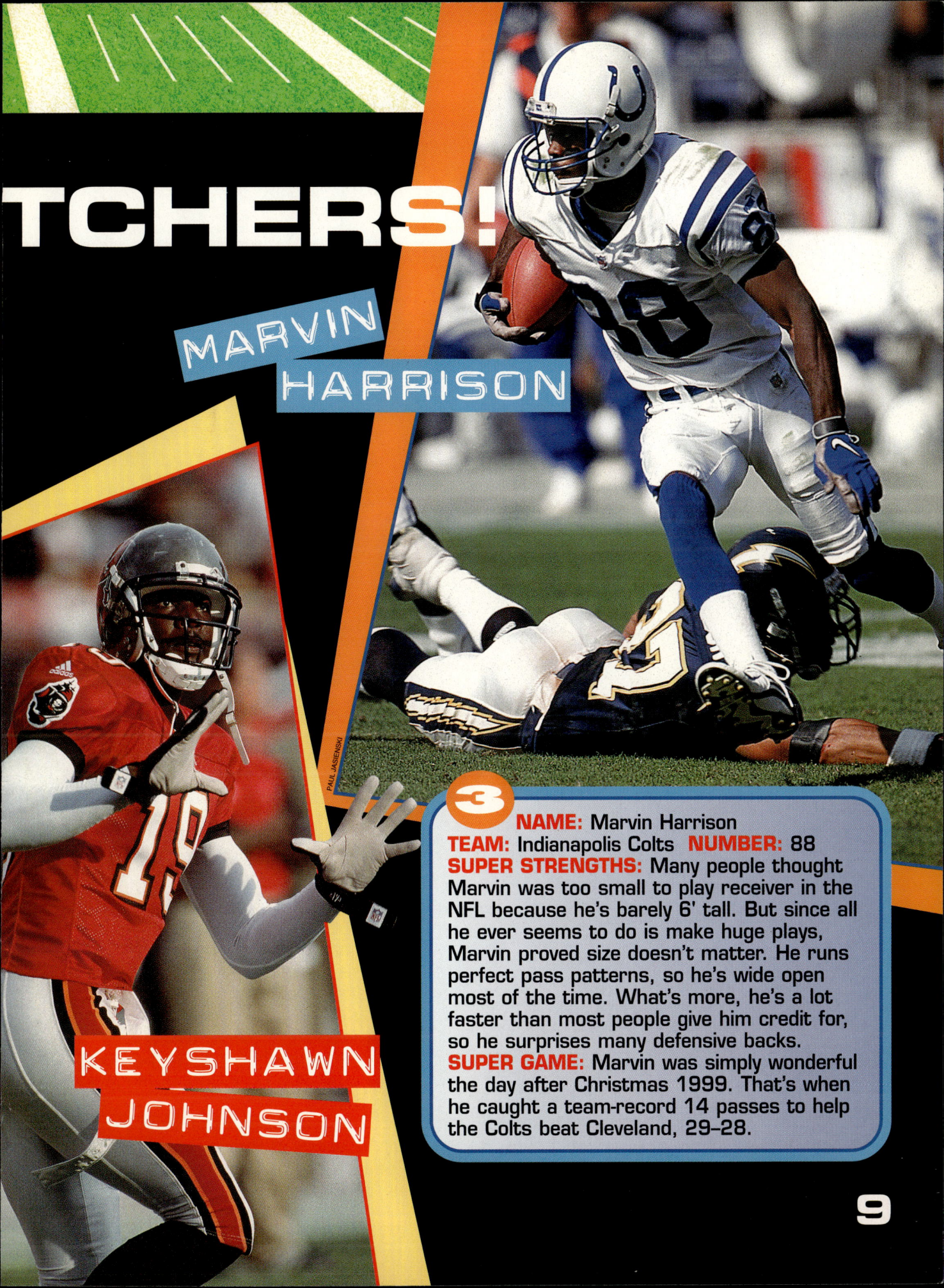

MARVIN HARRISON

KEYSHAWN JOHNSON

3 NAME: Marvin Harrison
TEAM: Indianapolis Colts **NUMBER:** 88
SUPER STRENGTHS: Many people thought Marvin was too small to play receiver in the NFL because he's barely 6' tall. But since all he ever seems to do is make huge plays, Marvin proved size doesn't matter. He runs perfect pass patterns, so he's wide open most of the time. What's more, he's a lot faster than most people give him credit for, so he surprises many defensive backs.
SUPER GAME: Marvin was simply wonderful the day after Christmas 1999. That's when he caught a team-record 14 passes to help the Colts beat Cleveland, 29–28.

SUPER PLAYERS!
SUPER RUNNERS!

MARSHALL FAULK

② NAME: Marshall Faulk
TEAM: St. Louis Rams **NUMBER:** 28
SUPER STRENGTHS: Marshall is a rare superstar because, in addition to being one of the best running backs in the league, he can catch the ball like a receiver. His versatility makes it nearly impossible for defenses to plan for him. That's why he breaks at least one big play in almost every game. Marshall's blazing speed is probably second among his list of qualities, right behind his jaw-dropping moves.
SUPER GAME: Although Marshall ran for just 17 yards in Super Bowl XXXIV, he helped the Rams win by catching five passes for 90 big yards.

PETER READ MILLER/SPORTS ILLUSTRATED

EDDIE GEORGE

1

NAME: Eddie George
TEAM: Tennessee Titans **NUMBER:** 27
SUPER STRENGTHS: Most football experts agree that Eddie has the perfect physique (6-foot-3, 240 pounds) for an NFL running back. His chiseled upper body and mammoth legs make for an unstoppable combination. He can run faster than defenders, and he can run over them. Eddie is so strong that one defender rarely can bring him down, and he dishes out as much punishment as he receives. His upright running style is an awesome sight.
SUPER GAME: Eddie turned in a marvelous performance in Super Bowl XXXIV, rushing for two touchdowns and 95 yards. He also caught two passes for 35 yards.
SUPER STAT: George rushed for 1,304 yards in 1999, third best in the AFC. He also had 458 receiving yards.

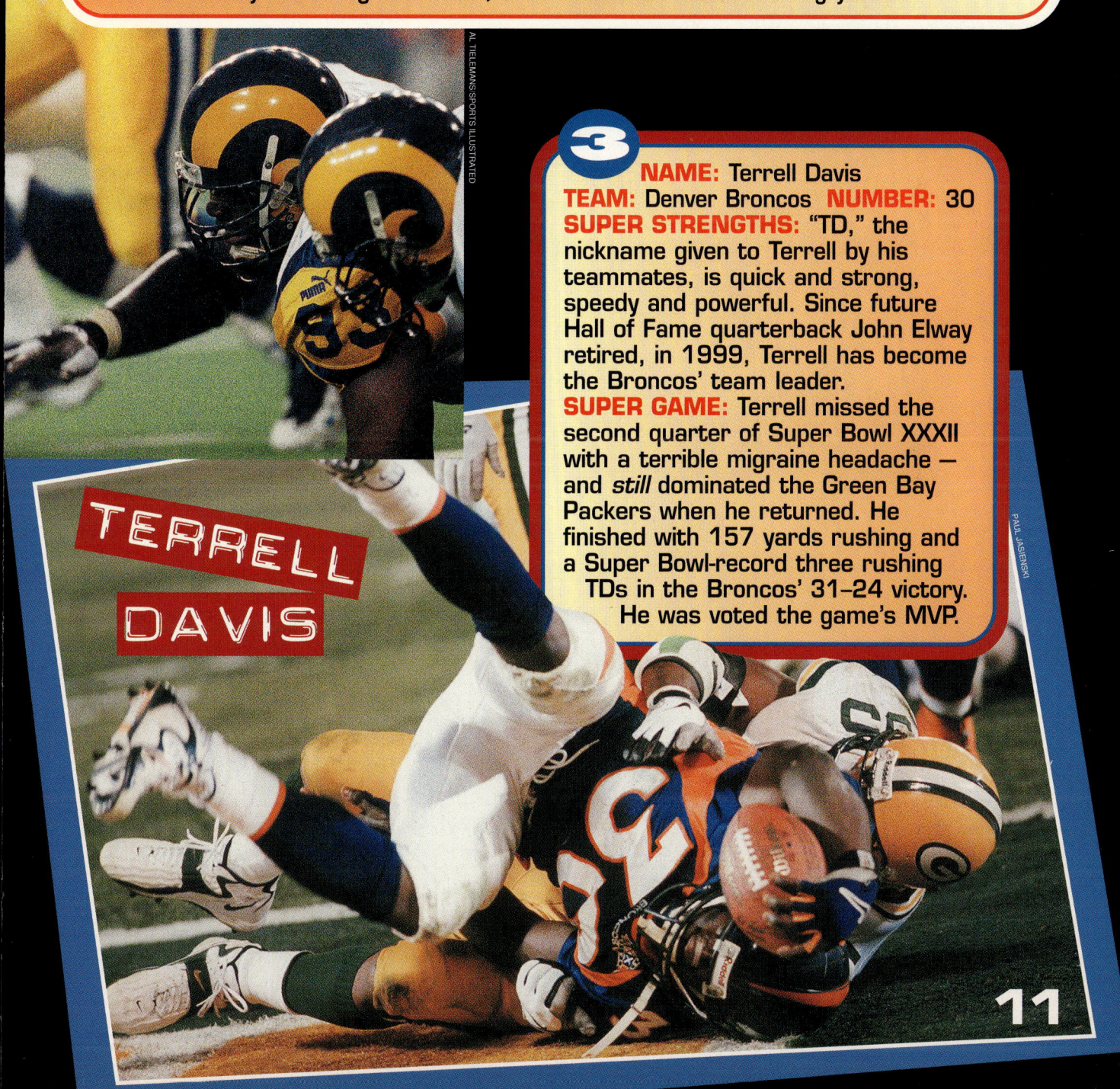

TERRELL DAVIS

3

NAME: Terrell Davis
TEAM: Denver Broncos **NUMBER:** 30
SUPER STRENGTHS: "TD," the nickname given to Terrell by his teammates, is quick and strong, speedy and powerful. Since future Hall of Fame quarterback John Elway retired, in 1999, Terrell has become the Broncos' team leader.
SUPER GAME: Terrell missed the second quarter of Super Bowl XXXII with a terrible migraine headache — and *still* dominated the Green Bay Packers when he returned. He finished with 157 yards rushing and a Super Bowl-record three rushing TDs in the Broncos' 31–24 victory. He was voted the game's MVP.

SUPER PLAYERS!
SUPERs

JEVON KEARSE

1
NAME: Jevon Kearse
TEAM: Tennessee Titans
NUMBER: 90
SUPER STRENGTHS: You want to know why Jevon's nickname is "The Freak"? Well, he's a defensive lineman with the speed of a wide receiver, the vertical jump (40 inches) and wingspan (86 inches) of a basketball player, and hands that look as if they were a foot long! He can play any position along the front line, but he can also drop back and provide help in pass coverage.
SUPER GAME: During a regular-season game against the St. Louis Rams in 1999, Jevon was all over the field, getting one sack, forcing a fumble, and making five tackles in the Titans' 24–21 victory.
SUPER STAT: Jevon recorded a rookie-record 14 quarterback sacks in 1999 in becoming the NFL's Defensive Rookie of the Year.

TOM DIPACE

3
NAME: Deion Sanders
TEAM: Washington Redskins **NUMBER:** 21
SUPER STRENGTHS: Deion, nicknamed "Neon" for his flashy style of play, is one of the greatest cornerbacks in the history of professional football. Many experts believe that he is the fastest player in the NFL. That blistering speed enables Deion to do things other than play defense. He can play receiver, he can run the ball, and he's one of the best kick returners of all time.
SUPER GAME: In Dallas's Super Bowl XXX win over the Pittsburgh Steelers, Deion caught a 47-yard pass from Troy Aikman to become the only player in Super Bowl history with both an interception and a pass reception.

TOPPERS!

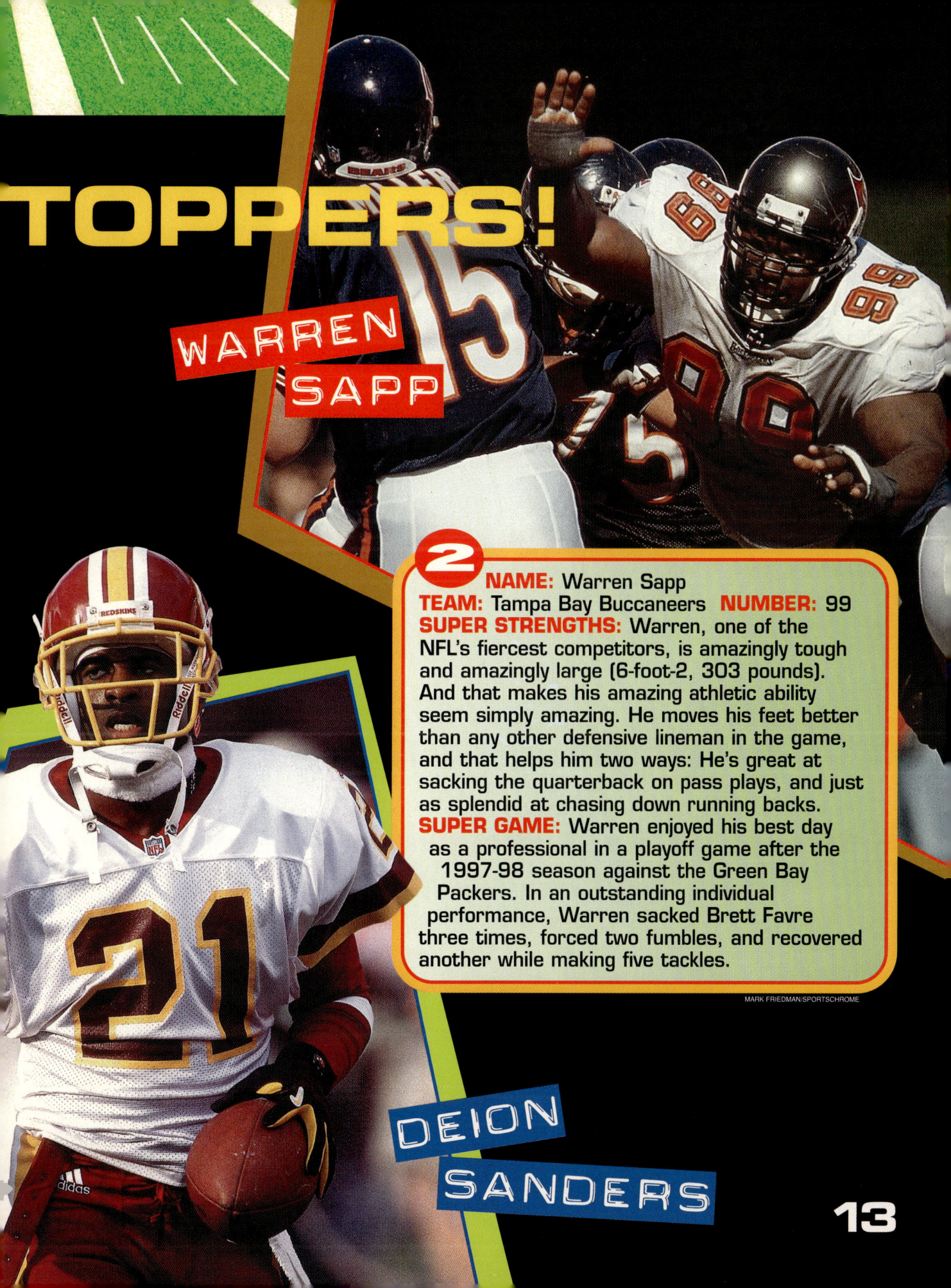

WARREN SAPP

2

NAME: Warren Sapp
TEAM: Tampa Bay Buccaneers **NUMBER:** 99
SUPER STRENGTHS: Warren, one of the NFL's fiercest competitors, is amazingly tough and amazingly large (6-foot-2, 303 pounds). And that makes his amazing athletic ability seem simply amazing. He moves his feet better than any other defensive lineman in the game, and that helps him two ways: He's great at sacking the quarterback on pass plays, and just as splendid at chasing down running backs.
SUPER GAME: Warren enjoyed his best day as a professional in a playoff game after the 1997-98 season against the Green Bay Packers. In an outstanding individual performance, Warren sacked Brett Favre three times, forced two fumbles, and recovered another while making five tackles.

MARK FRIEDMAN/SPORTSCHROME

DEION SANDERS

SUPER TEAMS!

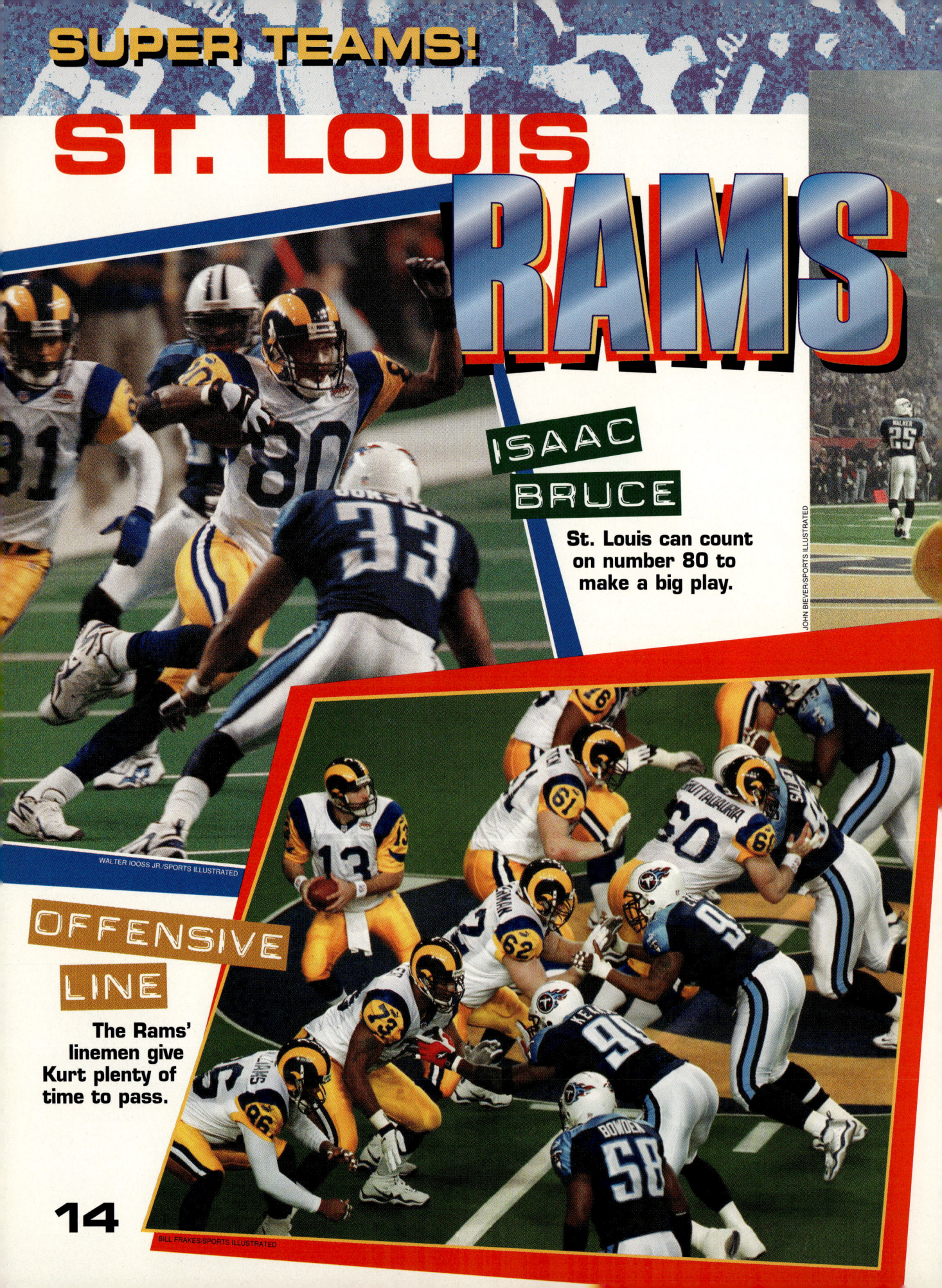

ST. LOUIS RAMS

ISAAC BRUCE
St. Louis can count on number 80 to make a big play.

OFFENSIVE LINE
The Rams' linemen give Kurt plenty of time to pass.

TOUCHDOWN DANCE

The Rams showed off their dance routine in Super Bowl XXXIV.

LAST SUPER BOWL VICTORY: Super Bowl XXXIV in 2000
SUPER STRENGTHS: The Rams have one of the most explosive offenses in the NFL. It's led by quarterback Kurt Warner, running back Marshall Faulk, and wide receiver Isaac Bruce. Their quick-strike passing game relies mostly on the team's overall great speed. This offense enables St. Louis to score from anywhere on the field.

The Rams' defense is aggressive and intent on attacking the other team. The Rams' defense and special teams also have a knack for creating their own scoring opportunities. During the 1999 season, the Rams led the NFC with 11 defensive and special-team touchdowns.

SUPER GAME: Super Bowl XXXIV had the most exciting finish in Super Bowl history. The Rams were leading the Tennessee Titans, 23–16, with six seconds left in the game. The Titans had the ball at the Rams' 10-yard line. Titan QB Steve McNair fired a laser-like pass to receiver Kevin Dyson at the Rams' three-yard line. As Kevin headed to the end zone, Ram linebacker Mike Jones tackled him one yard short as time ran out! For the first time, a Super Bowl was decided on the last play of the game.
SUPER STAT: St. Louis scored 526 points on the way to Super Bowl XXXIV, the third-highest total in NFL history. That's an average of almost 33 points per game!

SUPER TEAMS!

TENNESSEE TITANS

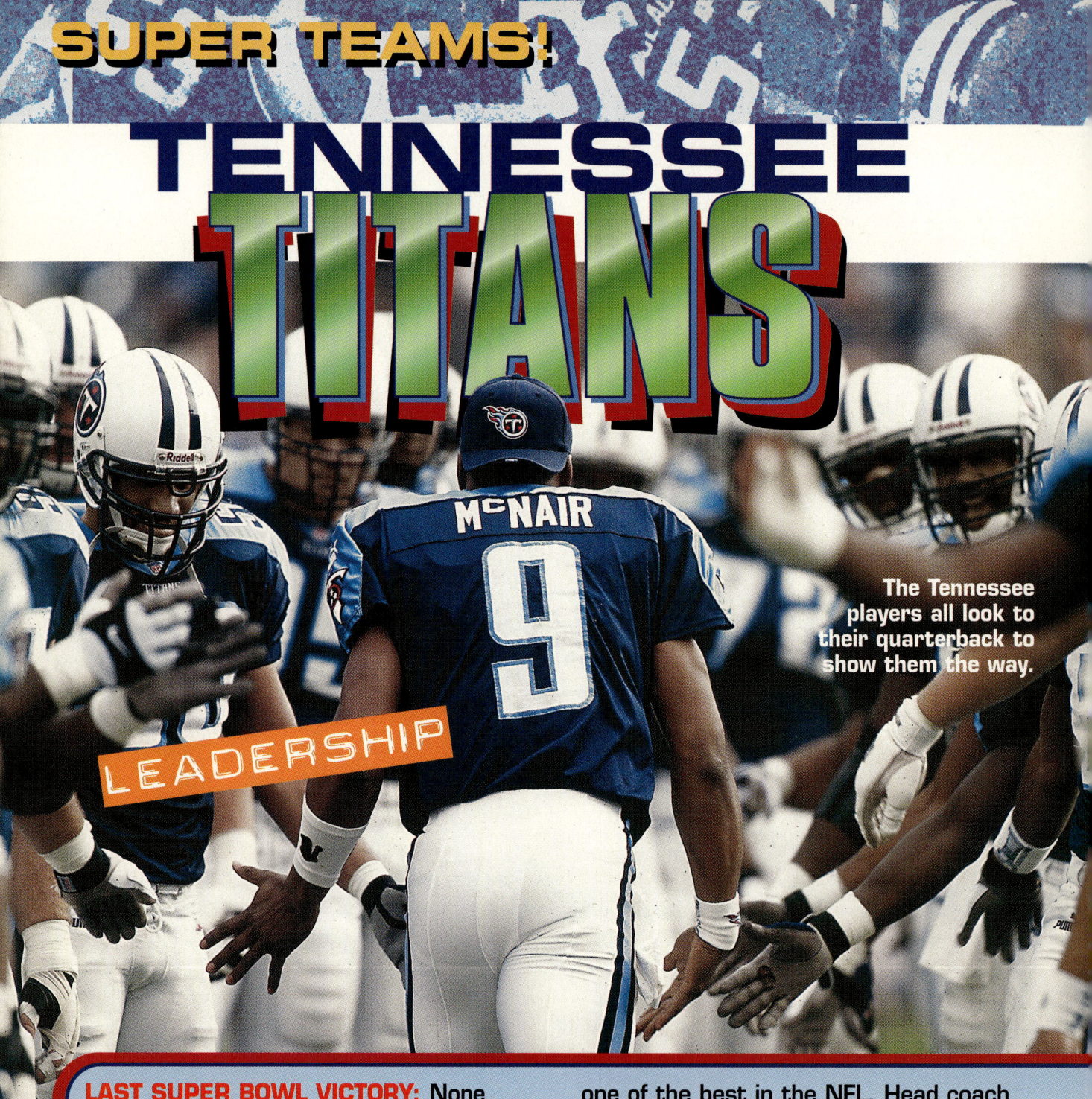

LEADERSHIP

The Tennessee players all look to their quarterback to show them the way.

LAST SUPER BOWL VICTORY: None
SUPER STRENGTHS: The Titans are driven on offense by their workhorse running back, Eddie George, one of the strongest players in the NFL. They repeatedly hand off to Eddie and let him bash the opposing defense until it's worn down. Then, Titan quarterback Steve McNair takes advantage of his ability to either throw downfield *or* run the ball like a running back. On the other side of the ball, Tennessee's defense is regarded as one of the best in the NFL. Head coach Jeff Fisher was the team's defensive coordinator before he became its coach.
SUPER GAME: It was the middle of the third quarter during Super Bowl XXXIV and Tennessee was losing to St. Louis, 16–0. Things were looking gloomy for the Titans. But they responded with a thrilling comeback. First, Eddie George scored one touchdown. Then he scored another. Finally, Titan kicker Al Del Greco booted a 43-yard field goal. Just like

The Titans were one of the few teams to contain Ram runner Marshall Faulk.

SWARMING DEFENSE

STEVE McNAIR

Steve is a good passer, but he can also run when he needs to.

that, the game was tied, 16–16! The Titans made Super Bowl history with that comeback. They were the first team ever to overcome a 16-point disadvantage.
SUPER STAT: The Titans were the only team to defeat the Jacksonville Jaguars, one of the best teams in the NFL, during the 1999 season. They beat Jacksonville twice in the regular season and then again when it mattered most — in the American Football Conference championship game.

17

SUPER TEAMS!

EDGERRIN JAMES

INDIANAPOLIS COLTS

Edgerrin's running style strikes fear in the hearts of opposing defenses.

LAST SUPER BOWL VICTORY: Super Bowl V, in 1971

SUPER STRENGTHS: Much like the St. Louis Rams, the Colts count on three skilled players to direct one of the league's most powerful offenses. Quarterback Peyton Manning, running back Edgerrin James, and wide receiver Marvin Harrison form a deadly one-two-three combination that usually knocks out any defense that gets in the way! The Colts win most of their games by scoring points in bunches, but their defense can be strong in the clutch.

SUPER SEASON: The Colts' "triplets" had a superb season in 1999. Peyton led the AFC in passing, Edgerrin led the AFC in rushing, and Marvin led the AFC in receiving yards and touchdown catches. All three started in the 2000 Pro Bowl.

MARVIN HARRISON

JACKSONVILLE JAGUARS

Mark and Fred give Jacksonville a great 1-2 punch.

MARK BRUNELL

FRED TAYLOR

LAST SUPER BOWL VICTORY: None
SUPER STRENGTHS: In six short seasons, the Jaguars have made huge strides from expansion team to the top of the NFL. Here's how they did it: They found Mark Brunell, a left-handed Pro Bowl quarterback who's as mobile as any running back in the game. Then, they built a defense that could stop Godzilla if it had to. Finally, they drafted running back Fred Taylor, a sweet mix of moves, speed, and power who can take the ball all the way in the time it takes the opposition to say "Oh, no."
SUPER GAME: The Jaguars shocked football fans by defeating the powerful Denver Broncos in a 1996 divisional playoff game, 30–27. That game still is considered one of the biggest upsets in NFL history! The victory sent Jacksonville into the AFC championship game in just its second season, the fastest any expansion team had ever accomplished such a feat.

Marvin may not be as tall as some receivers, but he's just as dangerous.

SUPER TEAMS!
TAMPA BAY BUCCANEERS

Tampa Bay's line always gives it their all, on defense and on special teams.

WARRICK DUNN

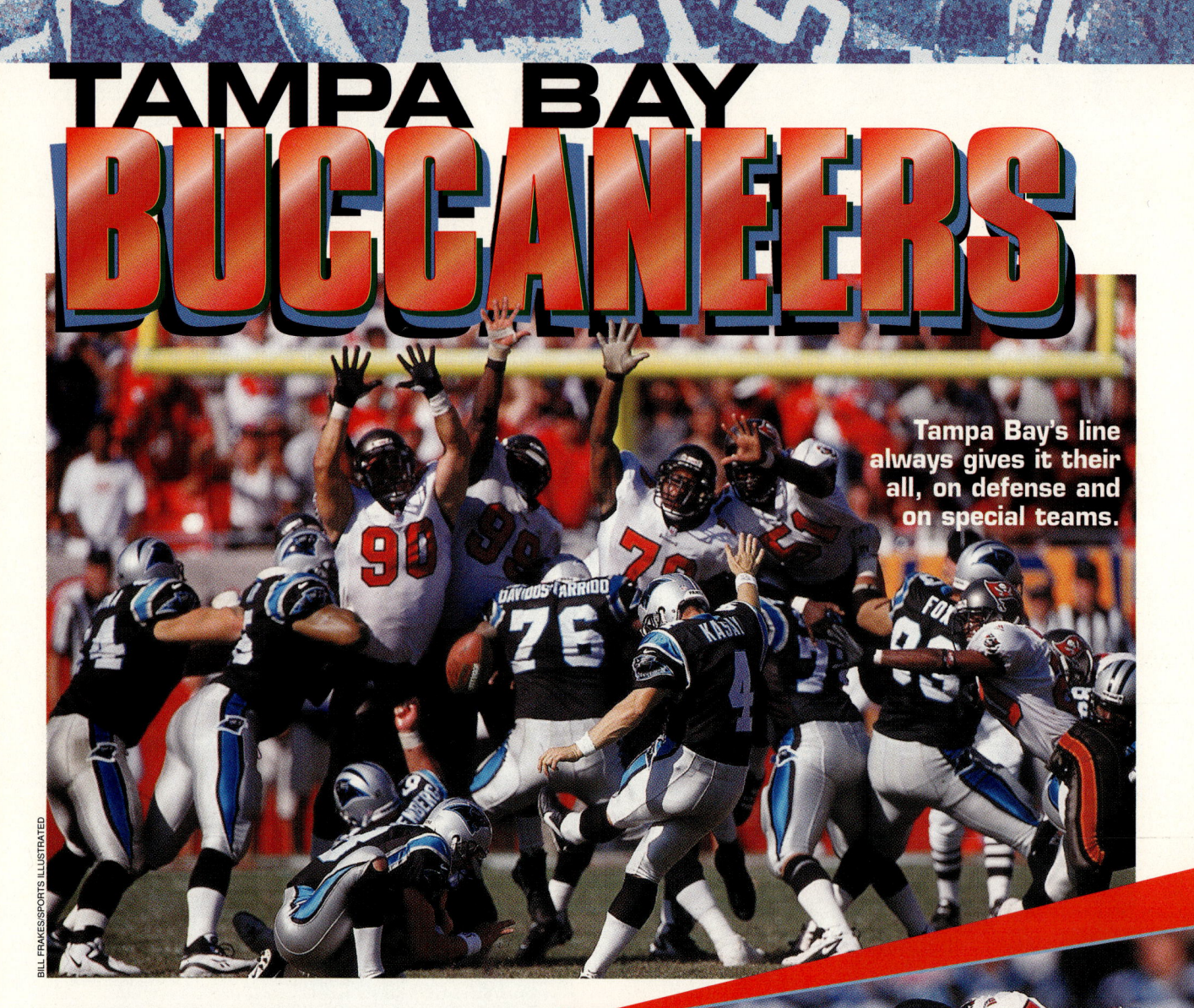

LAST SUPER BOWL VICTORY: None
SUPER STRENGTHS: Known as one of the fiercest defensive teams in the NFL, the Buccaneers are anchored by huge defensive tackle Warren Sapp and hard-hitting linebacker Derrick Brooks. On the other side of the ball, Tampa Bay has standout wide receiver Keyshawn Johnson and a two-headed monster in the backfield — the shifty, speedy Warrick Dunn and the big, bruising Mike Alstott.
SUPER SEASON: In 1999, the Bucs won eight of their last nine regular-season games to win the NFC Central Division title. Tampa Bay finished with 11 wins on the season, the most in team history.

When Brad goes back to pass, he must choose between some good receivers.

BRAD JOHNSON

JOHN BIEVER/SPORTS ILLUSTRATED

WASHINGTON REDSKINS

LAST SUPER BOWL VICTORY: Super Bowl XXVI, in 1992
SUPER STRENGTHS: Cornerback Deion Sanders and defensive end Bruce Smith lead the Redskins on defense. The two future Hall of Famers give the team one of the most talented defenses in football. It already had a good offense. Veteran Brad Johnson is the quarterback. He is assisted by running back Stephen Davis and big-play receivers Michael Westbrook and Albert Connell.
SUPER GAME: In Super Bowl XXVI, Redskin quarterback Mark Rypien passed for 292 yards and two touchdowns in Washington's 37–24 victory over the Buffalo Bills. Mark was named the game's MVP.

Warrick is extremely hard for defenders to get a handle on.

21

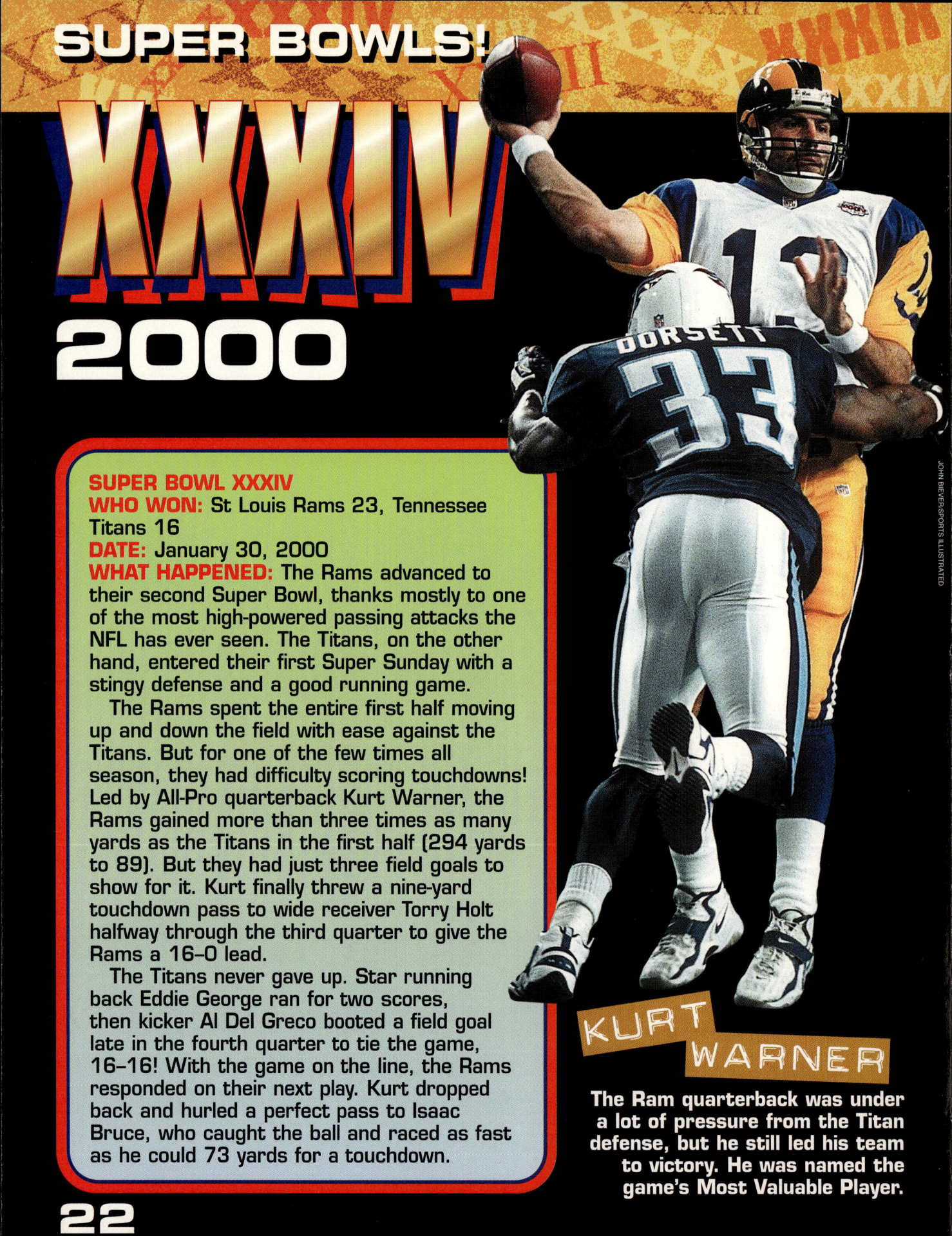

SUPER BOWLS!

XXXIV
2000

SUPER BOWL XXXIV
WHO WON: St Louis Rams 23, Tennessee Titans 16
DATE: January 30, 2000
WHAT HAPPENED: The Rams advanced to their second Super Bowl, thanks mostly to one of the most high-powered passing attacks the NFL has ever seen. The Titans, on the other hand, entered their first Super Sunday with a stingy defense and a good running game.

The Rams spent the entire first half moving up and down the field with ease against the Titans. But for one of the few times all season, they had difficulty scoring touchdowns! Led by All-Pro quarterback Kurt Warner, the Rams gained more than three times as many yards as the Titans in the first half (294 yards to 89). But they had just three field goals to show for it. Kurt finally threw a nine-yard touchdown pass to wide receiver Torry Holt halfway through the third quarter to give the Rams a 16–0 lead.

The Titans never gave up. Star running back Eddie George ran for two scores, then kicker Al Del Greco booted a field goal late in the fourth quarter to tie the game, 16–16! With the game on the line, the Rams responded on their next play. Kurt dropped back and hurled a perfect pass to Isaac Bruce, who caught the ball and raced as fast as he could 73 yards for a touchdown.

KURT WARNER

The Ram quarterback was under a lot of pressure from the Titan defense, but he still led his team to victory. He was named the game's Most Valuable Player.

JOHN BIEVER/SPORTS ILLUSTRATED

BATTLE LINES

Both the Rams and the Titans were determined to win their first ever NFL championship.

ANTHONY NESTE/SPORTSCHROME

Isaac grabbed the winning pass. It was a long bomb just over the defender's head.

GAME BREAKER

WALTER IOOSS JR./SPORTS ILLUSTRATED

SUPER BOWLS!

XXXIV
2000

FANTASTIC FINISH

Kevin Dyson caught a pass with just a few seconds left on the clock. As Ram linebacker Mike Jones tackled him, Kevin tried to put the ball into the end zone (1). But he couldn't reach it (2). He was down before he reached the goal line (3). The Rams won!

24

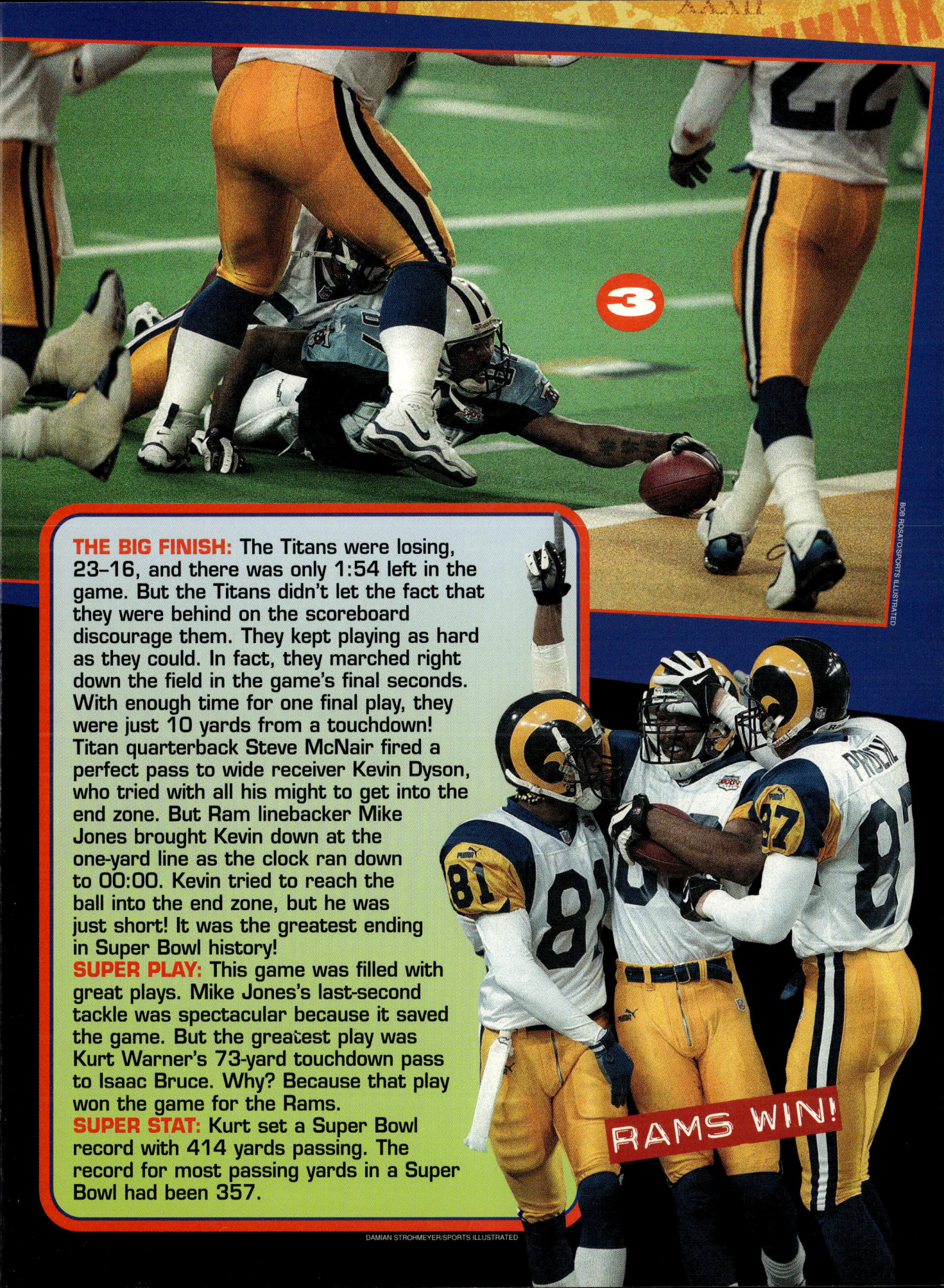

THE BIG FINISH: The Titans were losing, 23–16, and there was only 1:54 left in the game. But the Titans didn't let the fact that they were behind on the scoreboard discourage them. They kept playing as hard as they could. In fact, they marched right down the field in the game's final seconds. With enough time for one final play, they were just 10 yards from a touchdown! Titan quarterback Steve McNair fired a perfect pass to wide receiver Kevin Dyson, who tried with all his might to get into the end zone. But Ram linebacker Mike Jones brought Kevin down at the one-yard line as the clock ran down to 00:00. Kevin tried to reach the ball into the end zone, but he was just short! It was the greatest ending in Super Bowl history!

SUPER PLAY: This game was filled with great plays. Mike Jones's last-second tackle was spectacular because it saved the game. But the greatest play was Kurt Warner's 73-yard touchdown pass to Isaac Bruce. Why? Because that play won the game for the Rams.

SUPER STAT: Kurt set a Super Bowl record with 414 yards passing. The record for most passing yards in a Super Bowl had been 357.

RAMS WIN!

SUPER BOWLS!

XXXII
1998

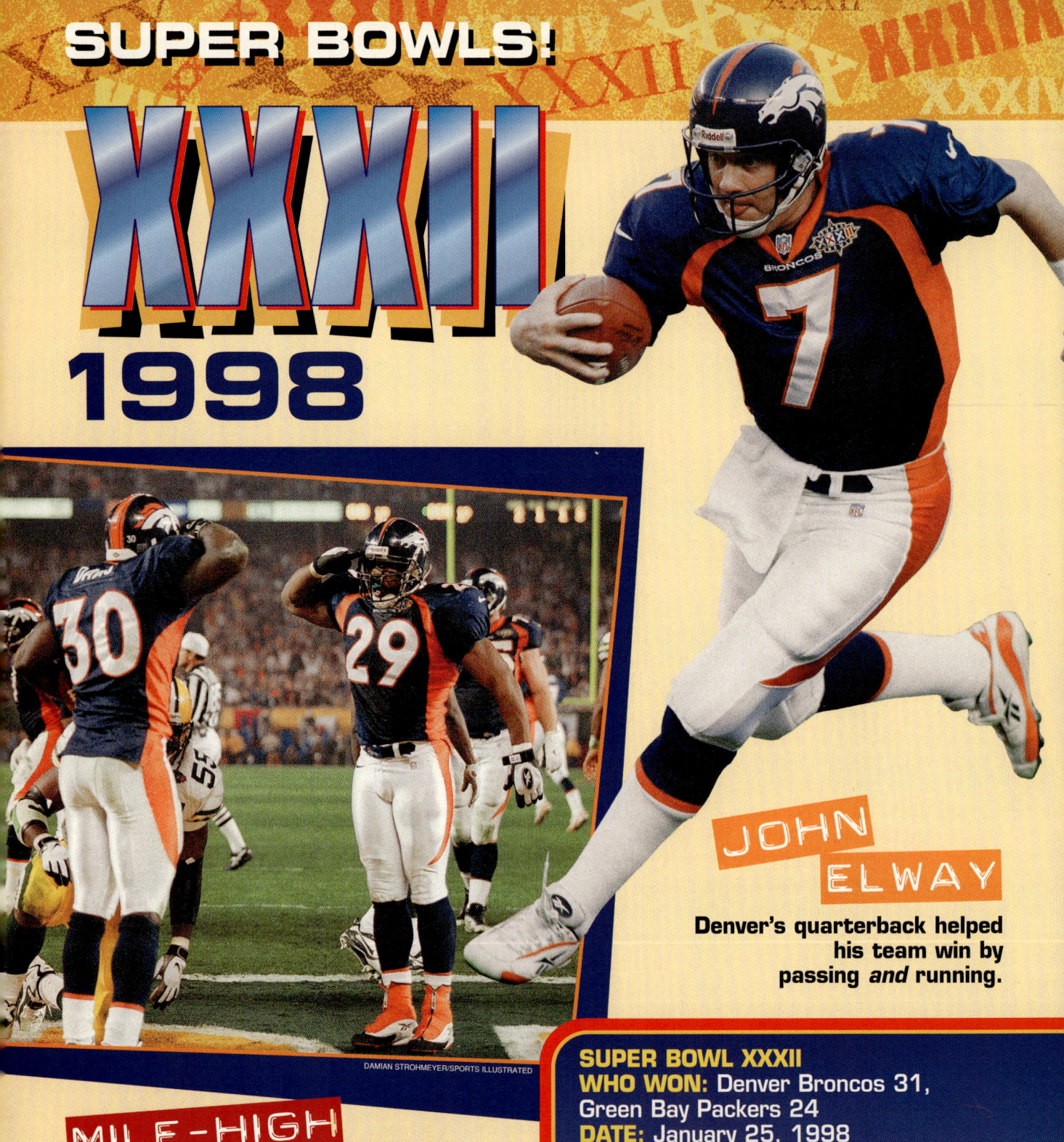

JOHN ELWAY
Denver's quarterback helped his team win by passing *and* running.

MILE-HIGH SALUTE
Denver is often called the mile-high city, so the Bronco players celebrated touchdowns with the mile-high salute.

DAMIAN STROHMEYER/SPORTS ILLUSTRATED

SUPER BOWL XXXII
WHO WON: Denver Broncos 31, Green Bay Packers 24
DATE: January 25, 1998
WHAT HAPPENED: After Green Bay scored to take a 7–0 lead, Packer turnovers helped the Broncos score 17 points in a row. Then, the game became a classic. The Packers scored the next 10 points to tie the score! But running back Terrell Davis's one-yard touchdown run with less than two minutes left gave the Broncos the win.

26

BRETT FAVRE

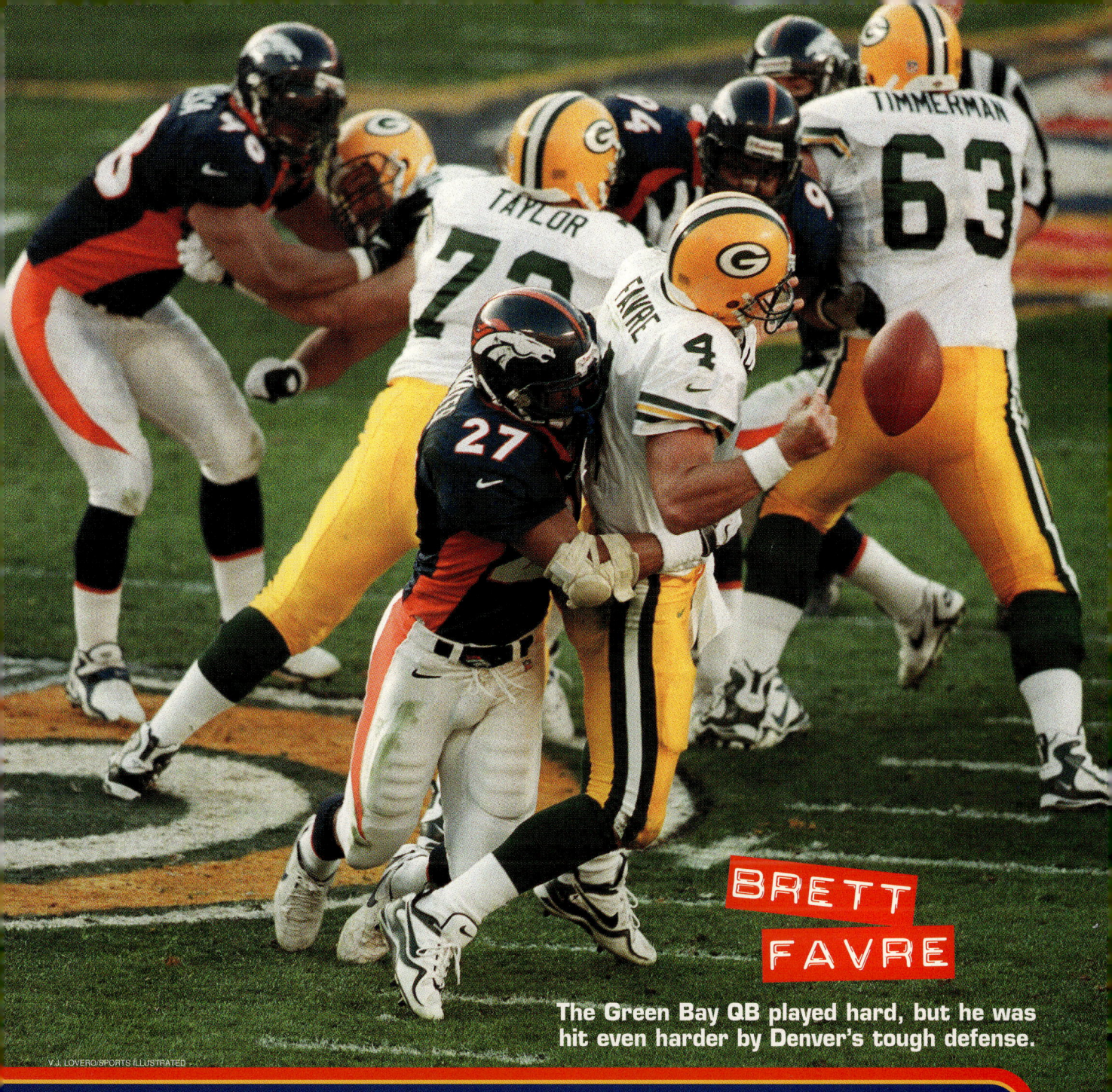

The Green Bay QB played hard, but he was hit even harder by Denver's tough defense.

SUPER PLAY: The game was tied, 17–17, late in the third quarter. The Broncos had a third down with the ball at the Packers' 12-yard line. They needed just six yards to get a first down. Legendary quarterback John Elway wanted to pass, but no one was open. He ran. At the last possible second, he leaped into the air, right at three defenders. The collision sent John spinning like a top. When he finally came down, the Broncos had a first down. Terrell scored two plays later.

SUPER STAT: Terrell Davis missed almost all of the second quarter with a painful headache. But that didn't stop him from winning the Super Bowl MVP trophy. He rushed for 157 yards and three of the Broncos' four touchdowns!

SUPER HISTORY: This game was the Packers' first Super Bowl loss in four tries. They won the first two Super Bowls, way back in the 1960's. For the Broncos, it was the first of two straight Super Bowl victories after four painful losses during the 1970's and 1980's.

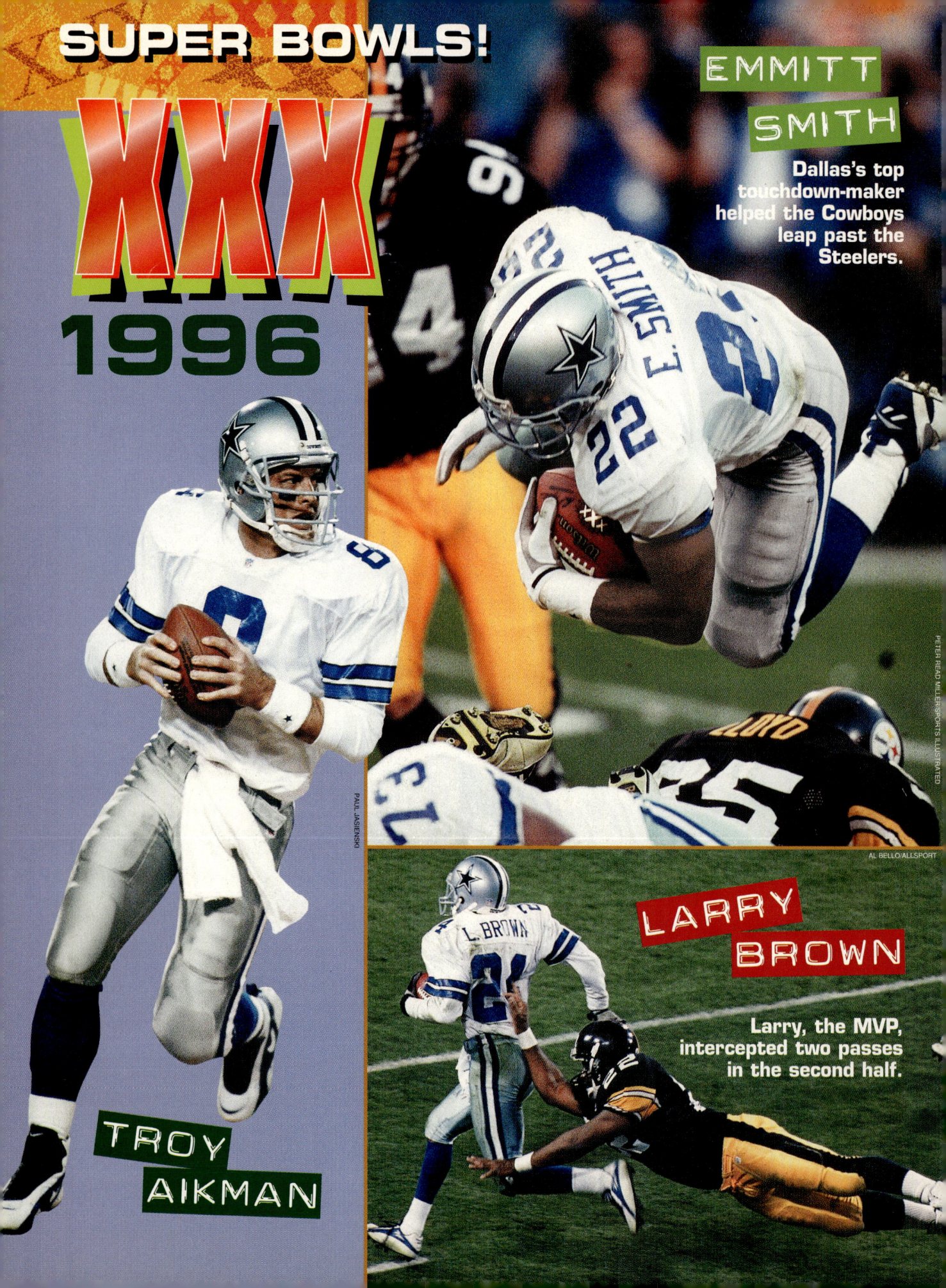

SUPER BOWLS!
XXX
1996

EMMITT SMITH
Dallas's top touchdown-maker helped the Cowboys leap past the Steelers.

TROY AIKMAN

LARRY BROWN
Larry, the MVP, intercepted two passes in the second half.

SUPER BOWL XXX

WHO WON: Dallas Cowboys 27, Pittsburgh Steelers 17
DATE: January 28, 1996
WHAT HAPPENED: The Cowboys and Steelers celebrated the Super Bowl's 30th birthday by meeting to decide the NFL championship for the third time. The Steelers won the first two games, in the 1970's. They wouldn't be so lucky the third time around! Dallas was leading at the half, 13–7. Pittsburgh played great in the second half, but suffered when quarterback Neil O'Donnell threw two costly interceptions. The turnovers helped Dallas hold on for the victory. It was the Cowboys' third Super Bowl triumph in a span of four years. No other team had ever done that!

SUPER PLAY: Cowboy defensive back Larry Brown was in the right place at the right time for two key interceptions in the second half. He returned the first one for 44 yards and the second one for 33 yards. The Cowboys went on to score touchdowns both times. For his effort, Larry was voted the game's MVP.

SUPER STAT: The Steelers had 10 more first downs than the Cowboys, 47 more rushing yards, 9 more passing yards, 1 less punt, and 3 fewer penalties. And they lost!

SUPER HISTORY: Between them, the Cowboys and Steelers have won nine Super Bowls. The Steelers won their four in the 1970's. The Cowboys won two in the '70s and three more in the '90s.

TOUGH DEFENSE

The Dallas defense held Pittsburgh running back Jerome Bettis (number 33) in check.

DAMIAN STROHMEYER/SPORTS ILLUSTRATED

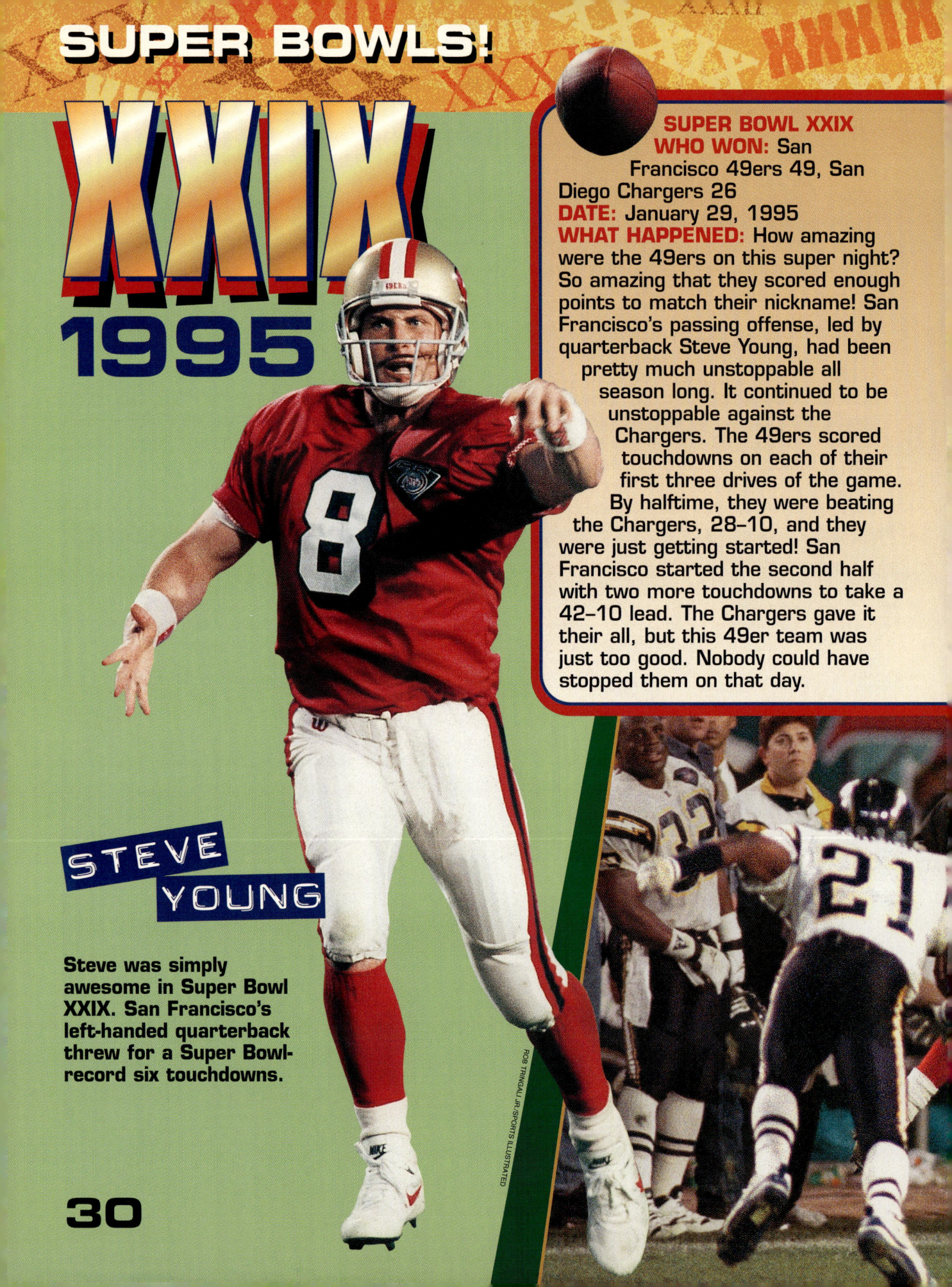

SUPER BOWLS!

XXIX
1995

SUPER BOWL XXIX
WHO WON: San Francisco 49ers 49, San Diego Chargers 26
DATE: January 29, 1995
WHAT HAPPENED: How amazing were the 49ers on this super night? So amazing that they scored enough points to match their nickname! San Francisco's passing offense, led by quarterback Steve Young, had been pretty much unstoppable all season long. It continued to be unstoppable against the Chargers. The 49ers scored touchdowns on each of their first three drives of the game. By halftime, they were beating the Chargers, 28–10, and they were just getting started! San Francisco started the second half with two more touchdowns to take a 42–10 lead. The Chargers gave it their all, but this 49er team was just too good. Nobody could have stopped them on that day.

STEVE YOUNG

Steve was simply awesome in Super Bowl XXIX. San Francisco's left-handed quarterback threw for a Super Bowl-record six touchdowns.

ROB TRINGALI JR./SPORTS ILLUSTRATED

XXXIV

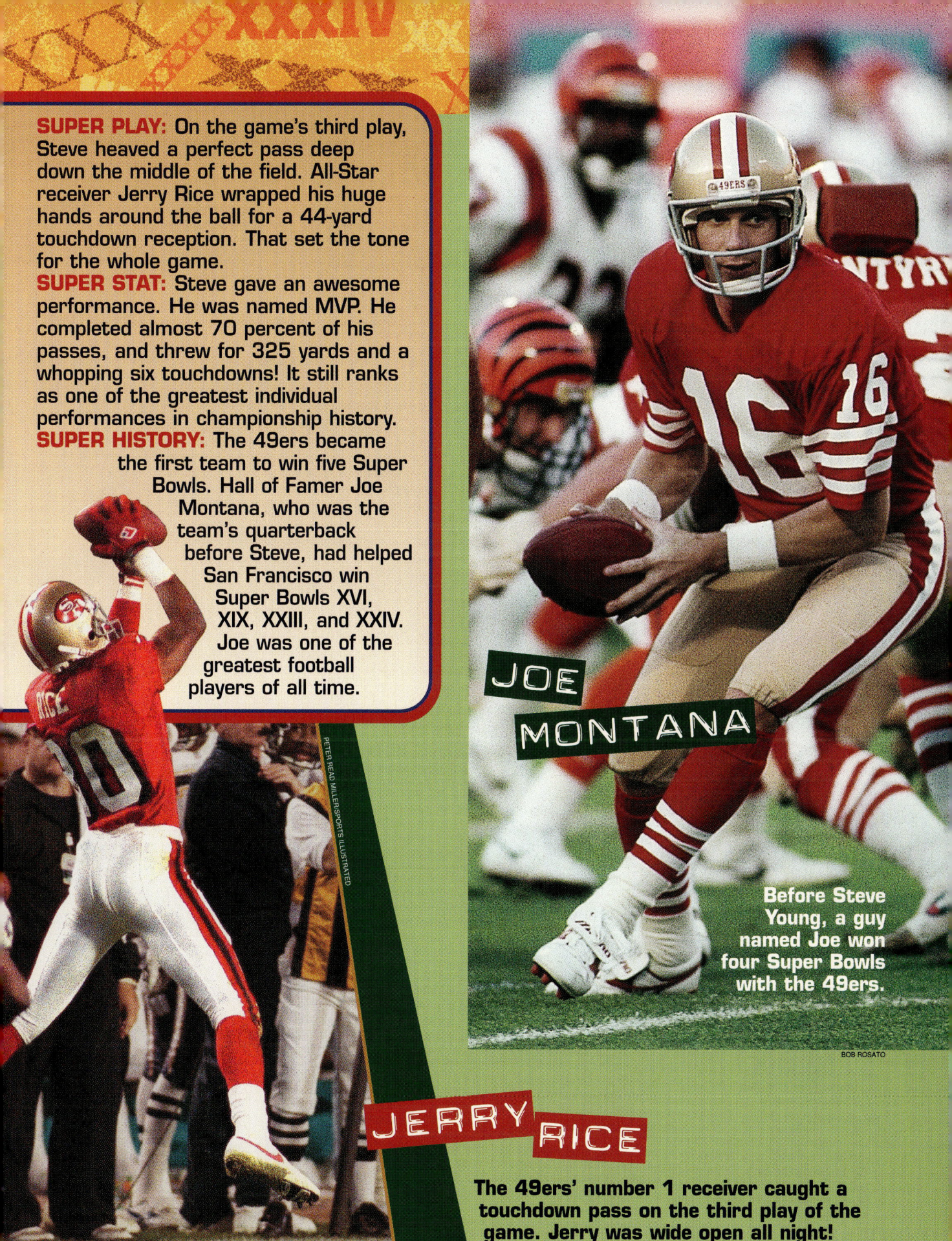

SUPER PLAY: On the game's third play, Steve heaved a perfect pass deep down the middle of the field. All-Star receiver Jerry Rice wrapped his huge hands around the ball for a 44-yard touchdown reception. That set the tone for the whole game.

SUPER STAT: Steve gave an awesome performance. He was named MVP. He completed almost 70 percent of his passes, and threw for 325 yards and a whopping six touchdowns! It still ranks as one of the greatest individual performances in championship history.

SUPER HISTORY: The 49ers became the first team to win five Super Bowls. Hall of Famer Joe Montana, who was the team's quarterback before Steve, had helped San Francisco win Super Bowls XVI, XIX, XXIII, and XXIV. Joe was one of the greatest football players of all time.

JOE MONTANA

Before Steve Young, a guy named Joe won four Super Bowls with the 49ers.

JERRY RICE

The 49ers' number 1 receiver caught a touchdown pass on the third play of the game. Jerry was wide open all night!

SUPER BOWL FUN FACTS

Here's the inside scoop on the NFL's greatest game!

🏈 In the very first Super Bowl, Green Bay Packer wide receiver Max McGee helped his team win by catching seven passes for 138 yards. Amazingly, Max had only caught four passes during the entire regular season! In the Super Bowl, he was filling in for an injured player.

🏈 For winning Super Bowl I, in 1967, each member of the Green Bay Packers earned $15,000. In 2000, each member of the St. Louis Rams earned $58,000 for winning Super Bowl XXXIV.

🏈 Until Super Bowl XXV, in 1991, the game's most valuable player received a watch. To help celebrate the Super Bowl's 25th anniversary, the NFL began awarding the Pete Rozelle Trophy to the game's MVP. Rozelle was the NFL's commissioner from 1960 to 1989. His job was to make the NFL just as popular as the other major sports, and he succeeded!

🏈 In 1980, 103,985 fans crammed into the Rose Bowl, in Pasadena, California, to watch Pittsburgh beat the Los Angeles Rams, 31–19, in Super Bowl XIV. The Rams are not in Los Angeles any more (they moved to St. Louis in 1995), but the crowd still ranks as the largest in Super Bowl history.

🏈 The sterling-silver trophy presented to the Super Bowl champion is named after Vince Lombardi, the Hall of Fame head coach who led the Green Bay Packers to victories in Super Bowls I and II. The trophy weighs seven pounds, stands 21 inches tall, and is topped with a regulation-sized silver football.

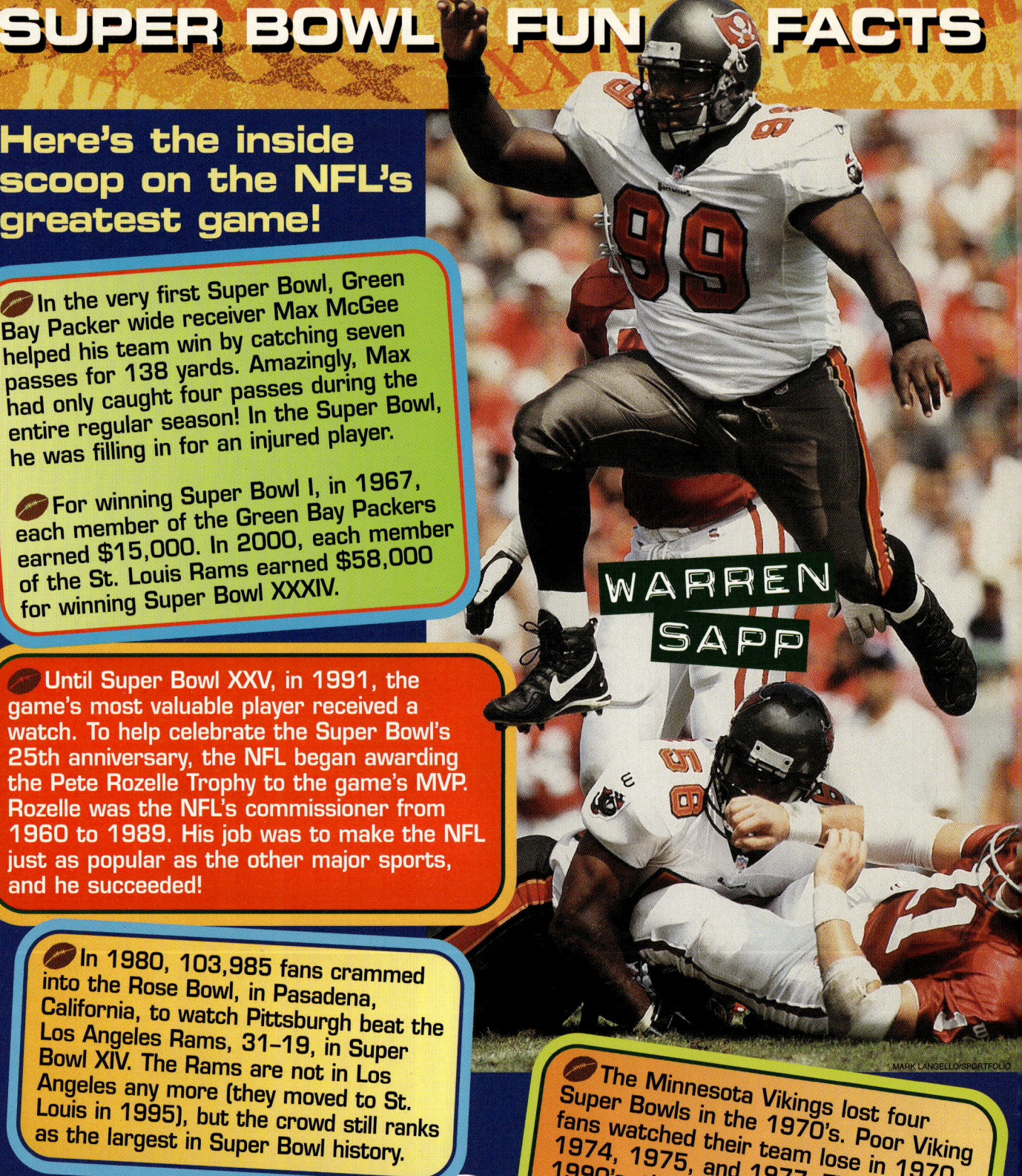

🏈 The Minnesota Vikings lost four Super Bowls in the 1970's. Poor Viking fans watched their team lose in 1970, 1974, 1975, and 1977. Then, in the 1990's, the Buffalo Bills lost four Super Bowls . . . in a row! The Bills lost in every Super Bowl from 1991 to 1994.

🏈 Don Shula, the legendary coach of the Dolphins from 1970 to 1995, coached in six Super Bowls, more than any other head coach.

WARREN SAPP

MARK LANGELLO/SPORTFOLIO